5113

Teaching 5 to 13
Reading

Word pack
skills

John Ireland
Adviser for Primary Education
Metropolitan Borough of Bury

Introduction by
Donald Moyle
Reader in Education
Edge Hill College of Higher Education

Macdonald Educational
London and New York

ISBN 0 356 05055 6

Published by
Macdonald Educational Ltd
Holywell House
Worship Street
London EC2

850 Seventh Avenue
New York 10019

Photographs : Terry Williams

Artwork : Eleanor Mills
Janet Jones

Cover design : Peter Gauld

Cover photograph : Henry Grant

The author and publishers gratefully acknowledge the help given by the following :

The staff and children of Town Green County Primary School, Aughton, Ormskirk, Lancashire
Mrs E. Halliwell, Head Teacher, Mersey Drive County Infant School, Bury, Lancashire
Miss Anne Tunstall, Head Teacher, St Michael's R.C. Infant School, Bury, Lancashire
Mrs B. Brown, Assistant Curriculum Development Officer, Bury Teachers' Centre

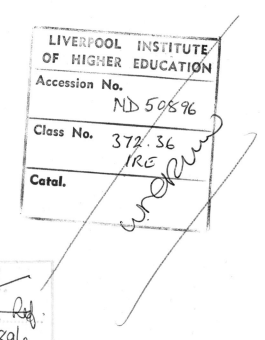
Made and printed by
Morrison and Gibb Limited, London and Edinburgh

Teaching 5 to 13

In recent years books for teachers have taken the title of 'guides'. These often provide the pedagogic background to new developments in education. There seems little point in adding another series to this well supplied field when perhaps the greatest need is for a range of books which will reflect current developments in education in severely practical terms. *Teaching 5 to 13* aims to do just this by providing sources of immediate help for teachers facing current developments in the classroom and who may be seeking a curriculum content and a teaching approach to meet new situations.

The age range from five to thirteen is the longest span in a child's educational life at school, now unhampered by the demands of external examinations. It is a period of the maximum flexibility at the teacher's disposal, when individual demands can take precedence over subject demands, when subjects can be treated in broad terms. However, there is also time for studies in depth, for the acquisition of skills and their application in the context of reality. The more flexible timetable accommodates these freedoms, but of course it equally puts new demands upon the teacher's resources. *Teaching 5 to 13* aims to give practical help in these situations by providing a sharing of experience by teachers who have worked in these situations for their colleagues facing similar experiences.

Most teachers want to see the results of innovations before introducing them into their own classrooms. Above all they would like to see the situations for themselves, but this is rarely possible. *Teaching 5 to 13* tries to meet this need in some measure by the liberal use of photographs of the actual situations described by the authors. Again, because the authors are practising teachers who are writing and sharing their experiences, this combination of picture and text gives an added integrity and reality. Another use is made of illustrations in the series which makes it significantly different from other books for

teachers. Where it is appropriate as much information as possible is given in the pictures and diagrams. This not only saves text and time, but also enables much more information to be put in context without overloading it with words. It also enables the authors to show exactly how they carried things through or organised them in the confines of the actual classroom with realistically large classes and groups.

The integrated curriculum and resource based education are phrases descriptive of developments into which many new approaches in education fit. However, they pre-suppose resources in terms of ideas, experience and organisation which the teacher busy with day to day demands may not necessarily have developed. *Teaching 5 to 13* aims to provide a view across the curriculum which places these ideas in context for those new to them, gives back-up help to those currently operating them and information for those planning to introduce them.

The range of books in the series will be wide enough to illustrate both changes in emphasis as well as curriculum content as the child develops over the years between five and thirteen. Equally this means that where it is appropriate subject strands in the curriculum will be treated as such. They will reflect new developments as well as incorporate the essential care of established practice. Mathematics will be treated so that the 'new maths' are not divorced from the traditional material and both are related to the realities of life in and out of the classroom. Environment studies on the one hand, will be used to illustrate the unity between themes in science, history and geography, whilst on the other, for teachers of older children, subject studies in their own right will be given support through books in the series *Teaching 5 to 13*.

Frank Blackwell
Advisory Editor Teaching 5 to 13

Contents

Introduction

A person who reads well and fluently is able to understand what an author means to say and will use his own experience both of language and life to help him in this task. Teaching the mechanics of reading alone is not enough. All teaching of reading must be related to the children's experience and to their knowledge of language.

This book emphasises the importance of using both whole word methods of teaching reading, and of phonic approaches, so that it provides a balanced approach to word identification skills. But it also emphasises the importance of the use of context in learning to read. Once a child can recognise that a word he cannot read must be a particular part of speech in order to fit into the sentence, or that it is probably a word he knows will suit the meaning of the sentence, he is well on the way to fluent reading.

For this reason it is important to make sure that the first stages of learning to read make all this clear by using words which relate to a child's immediate experience. The ideas for activities and games in this book aim to do just this. However, the book makes it clear that it is essential to show children how to use the 'clues' to unknown words that fluent readers use all the time. Context is one clue, but so is the shape of a word (its configuration) and so are the sounds which constitute it. The skills and knowledge involved in using these skills may have to be taught separately, but eventually they must be related to the whole reading process. An ability to read for meaning is a fundamental part of this.

Donald Moyle

1 Word attack skills

Word recognition

Many teachers begin by trying to establish the skill of recognising individual words. But it is essential that work which develops techniques for word attack should arise from a meaningful and useful base, and not be taught in isolation from the normal areas where reading is of value.

For example, very few five year olds have difficulty in recognising the words 'ice cream'. Surprisingly, very few reading schemes include these words and only one does so in the first reader. A child will remember the words 'ice cream' because he associates them with something he likes and because they are useful words to be able to read. Teachers should remember this, and be sure that as frequently as possible the more mechanical aspects of reading are taught against a background of experience and to some purpose which is obvious to the child.

What are word attack skills?

There are three groups of word attack skills. All three are used by the adult reader and all should be made available to the young reader as early as possible. These skills are recognition by context, recognition by configuration and the use of phonics.

Context clues

There are two major types of context clue, those arising from a knowledge of the construction of English sentences, and those which arise from the meaning of a passage.

By the time they are five, children have mastered a tremendous amount of linguistic knowledge. They know a

large number of words and most can talk to each other in at least simple sentences.

This knowledge of language must be used in the teaching of reading. Try reading a story to a child, but leave out the occasional word. The child will attempt to find the missing word. He may get it right, or he may suggest a synonym or a word which slightly changes the meaning. However even when he mistakes the meaning completely he will rarely use the wrong part of speech. He has already achieved a very good understanding of the sentence patterns of English. Encourage him to use this knowledge in his reading.

When an adult reads, he is scarcely conscious of words at all. He reads in sequences of meaning, referring to the actual words to confirm that what he had predicted would be said was really there. The young child is not nearly so proficient, but must be encouraged to use his own powers of prediction in the same way.

This use of meaning to guess an unknown word is not, of course, a foolproof approach. The child is being asked to predict the meaning of a sentence and then select a suitable word from his spoken vocabulary. He could select a synonym rather than the right word. This may work at the time, but it may set up a habit of using the two words concerned interchangeably, or he may always respond to one word with the other. Most teachers know children who consistently confuse words in this way, for example reading 'small' every time they meet the word 'little'.

A young child, however, can select a word which does not fit or which changes the meaning of the sentence as written by the author. In this case not only has he read the word incorrectly he has also mistaken the intended meaning.

Lastly, in certain cases context may be unhelpful as in the instance of proper nouns. For the very young child the ability to use context to discover the subject or verb of a sentence is limited.

Configuration
Configuration is an approach to word recognition which is based entirely on memory. To recognise a word in this way a child must have met the word before and must remember it. The memory can be of the complete pattern of the word,

Above: reading a familiar story to a group of children. The teacher occasionally misses out a word. Below: the children try to guess the missing word

But this is not the case with English, which cannot be read in this way. To be sure that he has chosen the right word, the reader will have to refer to both his knowledge of spoken language and the context in which the word occurs as well as the letter sounds which make up each word.

A knowledge of the relationship between sounds and letters and a technique for using them is most helpful, but used in isolation from other skills can lead to mistakes.

Using the three kinds of skills
Adults need all three groups of word attack skills in order to read effectively, so children also need development in all three areas at all levels of attainment.

The consequences of too heavy a weighting in any one of these areas in the early stages are as follows:

Configuration
Children have far too much to learn in the early stages, and so cannot easily remember all the words they read. Children will ignore small differences between words and this leads to confusion.

Phonics
Children gain the idea, difficult to dispel later, that English spelling is regular.

Children develop the habit of looking carefully at every letter, so making them slow and hesitant readers. They learn to read thinking that the process is about words alone rather than the ideas and information the author is trying to convey.

Context
This approach can be difficult as it taxes the child's ability to remember ideas in detail. He can guess a word, getting both the idea and the word wrong yet still feel he has achieved a correct result.

For the adult reader the order used in recognition of words usually starts with reference to meaning, moves on to trying to remember if the word is at all familiar and finally, if necessary, the reader looks for support from phonic analysis and synthesis. Though the child will from time to time have to undertake learning activities in one area only, we should ask him to take the same route as the adult when he is reading normally.

or of some of its significant features such as length, initial, or final letters, or some particular grouping of letters such as 'ttle' in 'little'.

A child cannot expand his vocabulary by the use of configuration only. He must have someone to tell him the word in the first place or he must deduce it from picture or context clues.

But recognition by this method is very important. The young child may find remembering words learned by their pattern somewhat easier than other approaches. The fluent adult, of course, recognises words mainly from memory, having met them in the past.

Phonics
This is a scientific approach to word recognition. Its aim is to associate the symbols (i.e. letters) by which the word is represented in print, to sound values in speech.

In a language in which each letter symbolised has a different sound, the reader would be able to tackle any word as soon as he had mastered the sound of each letter.

2   Using word attack skills

Before children can use any of the word attack skills outlined in the previous section they must have developed the thinking strategies appropriate to each and also have learned a number of relevant facts about language.

Teachers must provide suitable activities for the children which will help them to learn these things. This means of course that the teacher has to be aware of the nature of the learning task involved and the constraints that the method of teaching and the materials used may impose upon it.

All word attack skills draw on a certain area of knowledge and abilities in common, but also demand specific learning or call for a greater expertise in certain areas.

The common areas are:

1. Spoken vocabulary. The first words a child learns to read should already be part of his spoken vocabulary.

2. Meaning. A child must know that language is used to express messages which mean something.

3. Letters. Visual symbols represent speech sounds.

4. Words. A child should also know that language is broken down into units (i.e. words) and he must be able to recognise these units as part of his spoken language.

Operations used in recognition by configuration

When both children and adults recognise a word by its configuration, they do not necessarily look at the whole pattern of that word. They are much more likely to recognise a word in these ways:

1. By the initial letter or letters.

2. By the final letter or letters.

3. By some significant feature of the spelling pattern of the word.

4. By the length of the word.

Often two of these are used together. If a child uses (1) only the child might confuse 'green' and 'grass'. Using (2) only he may not distinguish 'say' and 'play'. In (3) the child would probably have problems with recognising the difference between words like 'little' and 'bottle'.

In order to recognise a word in this way the child must therefore:

1. Be able to notice the difference between the word he is reading and other words of similar pattern. In order to do this he must be able to notice letter shapes and be able to see the letters in their correct left to right order.

2. Be able to remember a visual image of the word.

3. Be able to relate the word he sees to his memory of spoken words and choose the right one.

If early reading instruction is based only on whole word teaching methods, children are bound to have to remember many different words and this can put a tremendous strain on the child's memory.

Operations necessary for recognition by phonics

Traditional teaching approaches to phonics ask the reader

to give single letters and letter groups a sound value. In order to do this successfully the reader must:

1. Be able to recognise letters accurately.

2. Be able to distinguish sounds within words.

3. Master a large number of generalisations concerning the spelling rules of English.

4. Be able to blend the sound units into a whole word sound.

The task of teaching reading in this way is a difficult one for the five year old unless it is broken down into stages. The task demands the ability to see and hear all the parts of a word and also the total word. Recent approaches have tended to simplify the learning task in two directions.

Firstly, the child is asked to learn the sound value of parts of words in relation to known words. So instead of a child being expected to tackle 'cat' by sounding out 'c-a-t' he is introduced to the word together with a picture:

Then still with the picture clue he is asked to supply the sounds which go to make up the words.

c–t   –at   ca–

Secondly, it may be helpful to ask a child to undertake only part of the total operation. For example, the teacher may do the analysis and the child the synthesis in both written and oral forms, e.g.

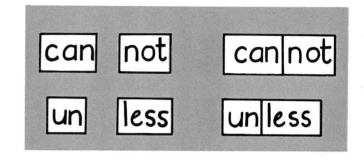

Operations employed in recognition from context

A reader may recognise a word in this way by working out what a sentence means from the words he already knows, and then picking out a word from his spoken language which fits into the total pattern of meaning. To do this successfully the reader must be able to:

1. Divide written language into meaningful idea units.

2. Work out what the author intended to say.

3. Read the relevant sections of a sentence after the unknown word as well as before it.

4. Have a knowledge of the grammatical structure of the language.

5. Hold the total idea the author is trying to convey in mind whilst trying to remember a word which fits into the gap.

But five year olds have short memories and a limited knowledge of language. Their ability to use trial and error techniques in searching for a word to fit a sentence is limited. It is necessary therefore to teach them that written language makes sense and that the real aim of reading is to think about the meaning of the words presented. Even the earliest reading materials must have meaning and purpose for a child if he is to use context clues.

3 Making a start: context and configuration

Many children come to school without any previous experience of the printed word. It is most important to show such children that the teacher finds reading useful, enjoyable and exciting. This will make them interested in learning to read. They must understand:

1. That the strange squiggles and shapes they can see on a page can be spoken and that they mean something.

2. That when we read words our eyes must travel across the page from left to right.

The background for this, it is hoped, will have been set by the parents reading stories with their own children. The teacher must continue this, partly because it will encourage children to want to read and partly to demonstrate the skills that the child is being asked to master.

A child cannot immediately learn to read a complete, worthwhile story for himself. The task must be broken down and support must be given. A young child must enjoy reading, and above all he must see it as useful.

Pictures and picture clues

Young children will enjoy simply looking at pictures but the activities listed below are designed specifically to encourage the development of:

1. Perception of the shape, orientation, colour and pictorial representation of familiar objects.

2. Children's understanding of how things happen, causes and possible effects. Children will understand why words are useful if they can understand the pictures.

3. Ability to use context clues.

4. Ability to predict events which are about to arise from any situation. This ability is used extensively in reading, as it overcomes the chore of looking at every letter in detail.

Matching and discrimination among pictures
Make some pairs of cards with illustrations of common objects on them. Ask the children to match these cards. When they have learned to do this they can use the cards to play 'Snap'.

Next, make some sets of cards which involve classification.

e.g. Animals and their young
Things you can ride
Things you can wear
Things you find in the kitchen

Make some story sequences where the pictures are placed on small pieces of card. Ask the children to arrange these in the right order.

Encourage children to think about the meaning of pictures and to learn to look for clues from all parts of the picture. Take a complex picture in which a lot of things are going on. Discuss this with the children and ask them to suggest what might happen. (Many pictures of this type appear in Macdonald Educational Zero Books.)

Vary this by presenting a serial in comic strip form like the one shown below.

Show a group of children the first picture in the strip, and then ask them to discuss it in this way:

'What do you think is going to happen?'

'Why do you think that will happen?'

'What is there in the picture that tells you that might happen?'

As successive parts are presented the children discuss the possibilities again.

7

If you use film strips while you tell a story this will introduce the idea that picture and language are inter-related. The film strip can be shown again while the children are telling the story themselves.

Ask the children to make their own picture books based on one of their favourite stories. At a later stage you can help them to add captions to make their own story books or comic strips.

Pictures and words

It is important that books within reading schemes have a text and pictures which are closely related. This is most helpful in the early stages of reading. Many of these books fail to have this relationship. Try making a system which involves recognition of familiar names of objects and colours. Make a line drawing with one part of the picture coloured. Write a caption for the picture. Children can learn very quickly that the one sentence caption contains the name of the colour and of the object coloured.

In the early stages it is helpful if work with books of this kind can be guided by a tape. The recording on the tape should be a discussion of the picture, drawing attention to its important features.

Eventually the tape should invite the child to read the caption together with the voice on the tape. The child can go through the book a number of times, if he wishes, before he reads it without the help of the voice on the tape.

Picture cards with word labels help to reinforce learning. Cards can be made self-corrective by using indentations. Later, use the same words and pictures without these.

Rhymes and context clues

Many young children do not know the common nursery rhymes which teachers probably expect them to have learned at home. This means that the teacher can introduce nursery rhymes to the children as something new.

Teach these at the same time as jingles and advertising slogans. Both are a source of vocabulary which will be helpful in the very early stages of reading.

Start by encouraging groups of children to recite and dramatise them.

They might make some illustrations for the rhymes.

When they have learned them children can play a game of fitting in missing words while the teacher recites the rhyme. The teacher should start by missing out the rhyming words, but go on to occasionally miss out other words.

The children can then move to a well-illustrated written version of the rhyme with words left out. Write these words on small pieces of card and ask the children to fit them into place. At first the children could do this using a tape recording to help them.

Children can make their own 'talking books' this way by taping the rhymes, making illustrations and then writing the text with words left out. Other children will supply these words when they read the rhyme. Make some joke books in the same way.

Children can gain valuable language experience from singing traditional songs and rhymes. Many of these involve finger exercises which help to develop both physical and mental co-ordination

Stories and context clues

One of the great difficulties in early reading is that the child has to work so hard to recognise words that he cannot enjoy their sense. This story method helps :

Tell the children a story, and be sure that it is told dramatically. A group of children might act the story out. Then ask each child to read a carefully illustrated version of the story. Knowing the story will help him to recognise many new words. This will give him a feeling of success and will teach him some new words.

Learning whole words and their configuration

When an adult reads, he remembers most of the words he comes across. It makes sense to provide young children with activities which will help them to build up a 'sight' vocabulary.

One of the easiest ways to introduce this will be to use the children's own names. Each name can be stuck over a coat peg. Provide a board in the classroom with name cards on, and use this to show who is responsible for each classroom task (see the photograph above).

It is helpful if the captions for objects and pictures are in the form of a sentence. Make matching cards in the form of the complete sentence, phrases, and individual words:

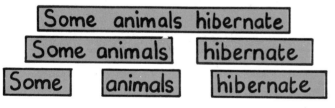

Help with word discrimination by using pictures. Ask the child to underline a word that describes the picture.

Discrimination without pictures
This exercise is to teach word discrimination without the help of pictures. Ask the child to draw a line under the word that is like the word in the box.

Christmas	holiday
	winter
	Christmas

snow	cold
	snow
	dark

fireworks	fireworks
	rocket
	banger

mother	father
	brother
	mother

Webster's Visual-Verbal approach helps children to learn words in relation to picture clues. This consists of cards with a single word overlaid on a picture. The picture can only be seen by holding the card up to the light. The idea is that the child attempts to read the word first. If he cannot, the child can use the picture. These cards can be used to play games on a point system. A child gets two points if he can read the word on its own and one point if he needs the picture to help him.

Starter clues

These exercises teach children to memorise words with a starter clue.

Put the labels on the picture.

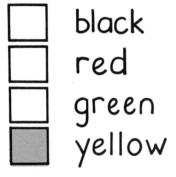

black
red
green
yellow

Put the right colour in these squares.

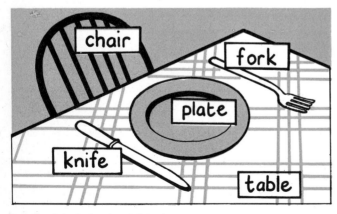

Put the labels in the right place.

Word banks

Word banks are more versatile than the picture dictionaries or word books which children often make in the early stages of reading. To begin with the child simply collects the words which he wants to use on cards.

If he uses punched file cards he can build them up with different kinds of systems of classification. There are a variety of ways to classify things. One way is by subject, e.g. flowers, clothes, parts of the body, colours, etc., another is by spelling pattern, e.g. words with 'ee'.

In the first case the words can be of considerable help in written work. In the latter, the teacher is given a store of base words which the child has used for phonic work.

The cards themselves can also be used as flash cards, for playing games, or for making up sentences. This is helpful to children who find writing difficult.

4   Phonic methods of word attack

Children will be helped to gain independence in word recognition if they know the relationship between sounds and symbols (letters) in English. But they will need plenty of background experience if they are to use these techniques successfully. The children must be able to recognise the shapes of letters immediately and relate these to the sounds within the words of their spoken vocabulary.

Is there an order for teaching phonics?

This is really two questions in one. Firstly, is there a best order for learning the spelling patterns of the sounds? And secondly, is there an order for the learning of the techniques of analysis and synthesis?

Spelling patterns
There are a number of possible ways of setting the order in which spelling patterns should be taught.

1. Sounds can be introduced in the order in which they appear in infant speech.

In the case of consonants this would result in: m, p, b, t, d, n, h, w, f, v, k, g, th, sh, zh, ch, j, s, z, v and l.

2. Other people believe that the child should learn the simplest and most regular spelling patterns first and then move on to the more complex and irregular. Within this area are a number of suggestions, for it is not always clear which spelling patterns are the more simple and regular.

One example is presented below. This is based on the idea that the most regular part of the language is to be found in single consonants at the beginning of words.

t, n, r, m, d, s, p, b, l, c, f, v, g, h, w, k, j, x, z, q, y.

3. A third suggestion is that the spelling patterns which should be taught first should be tackled in the order of the frequency in which they appear in written English. Again, there are two ways of approaching this. The order can be set by making a survey of a large amount of written English, representing all levels of reading ability. Alternatively the order could be set by examining the words a child himself uses at any given stage.

Experience suggests that there is no 'best order' of learning spelling patterns. What is important is that to become an effective reader the child must become acquainted with all spelling patterns. Teachers should make a check list so that they know all the patterns, and can be sure which each child knows.

A phonic check list

1. **Single consonants**
t, n, r, m, d, s, p, b, f, l, c.

2. **Short vowels**
a (bat), e (pet), i (pit), o (pot), u (hut).

3. **Consonant vowel combinations**
Present all the consonants and vowels shown above blended so that each consonant precedes a vowel.

4. **Final consonant blends**
nd, nt, ct, ng, ld, nk, rt, pt, mp.

5. **Consonant digraphs**
ch, th(thing), sh, th(this), wh, ph.

6. **Silent 'e'.**
cake, hope, kite.

7. Initial consonant blends
st, sp, sc, sk, sl, sw, sm, sn, pr, tr, gr, br, cr, dr, fr, pl, cl, bl, fl, gl.

8. Less frequent consonants
v, g, h, w, k, j, qu, x, y, z.
Alternate sounds of 'c' (cinema), s (pyjamas), g (gyrate).

9. Vowel digraphs
ai, ay, ea (eat), ee, ow (own), oa, ue (blue), er, ur, ir, ar, or, an (tank), aw, a (hall), ou (our), ow (now), oo (pool), oo (look), oi, oy, ea (head).

10. Double consonants
ll, rr, pp, tt.

11. Silent consonants
c (quack), k (knee), w (wrangle), p (psychology), h (ghost).

Techniques for analysis and synthesis

This is the side of phonics which involves skill. Knowing that certain letters represent certain sounds is of little value unless the child can recognise the patterns within words and then group them together. This task is quite complicated, and the child needs considerable practice at each stage in order to master this skill.

Exercises in analysis and synthesis

Letter recognition
You can make a dictionary word book which will give children the opportunities to get to know letters of the alphabet, and to learn to collect, sort and match word shapes. They can make their own dictionary.

It is important to keep the following points in mind when you are doing this:

1. That the sounds of letters are never taught in isolation.

2. That lower case letters should be taught separately from capitals.

3. That children need teaching how to form letters correctly and economically. These can be cyclostyled so that the children can trace over them.

Sounds in words
In order to use phonics the child must develop the ability to listen to sounds within words. Children very often do not know how many sounds there are in a word. If this is so the child should be allowed to listen to individual words very clearly enunciated.

Make boxes like the ones shown below. Ask the child to put counters in the spaces, one for each sound in the word. Notice that the number of sounds and the number of letters can be very different.

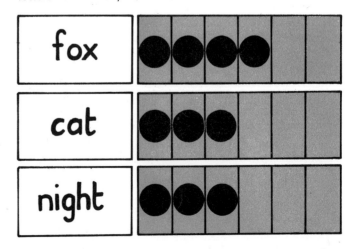

Find the stranger
Which of these words is the stranger? (Which of these words is out of place?)

Initial consonant: pot hat pin pan penny
                     man mother cat milk mug

Final consonant: mat sit big hut foot
                   rug dog big hit plug

Medial vowel: box hot frog sit lock

Rhyming
Choose a familiar nursery rhyme then ask the children to provide rhymes, e.g. Hickory Dickory dock, etc. Ask them to think of words which rhyme with 'dock'.

I spy
If you want to use this exercise to prepare the child for instruction in phonic skills this game should be played using letter sounds rather than letter names. Start by playing the game with a group of familiar objects displayed on a table. Once children are able to cope with this activity in a restricted area you can extend it to the whole room.

Sounds within sounds
Ask a child to respond when he hears a specific sound embedded in a background noise, e.g. a bicycle bell being rung during a peal of church bells. This will help him to discriminate between sounds.

Auditory sequencing and rhythm
Ask the children to do some of the following:

1. Repeat short sentences.

2. Repeat jingles and rhymes.

3. Listen to and obey commands.

4. Repeat the sequence of events in a story.

5. March and dance to simple rhythms.

6. Tap out rhythms or play percussion instruments.

Initial sounds
Some of this work should have already taken place as the children build up a vocabulary of words they know by sight. However, initial sounds will need to be taught more systematically. Here are some possible ways in which you can start:

1. Illustrate initial letter sounds by making cards. Put a drawing on one side of the card and the initial letter on the other.

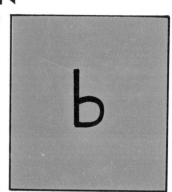

2. Prepare cards illustrating words children know by sight ('sight vocabulary'). Print the appropriate word under each picture. Ask the children to make the words using plastic letters.

3. Put pictures or objects into an envelope or bag. Ask the children to take them out and classify them according to the initial sounds of their names.

4. Cyclostyle a sheet of paper with pictures on it. Ask the children to repeat the exercise above, i.e. classify the pictures according to the initial sounds of their names.

5. Make cards with two columns of three words each. The child has to draw a line from one word on the left to a word on the right which begins with the same sound.

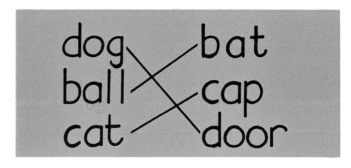

Final sounds

Some of the exercises for initial sounds can also be used in teaching final sounds, e.g.

1. Which word ends with the same sound as band?

rat, chair, bear, sound.

go, hen, round, kite.

parachute, candy, found, nest.

2. Phonic cards. Draw a picture on one side of a card. Write the name of the object in the picture under it, with the final consonant missing. Print the final consonant on the other side of the card.

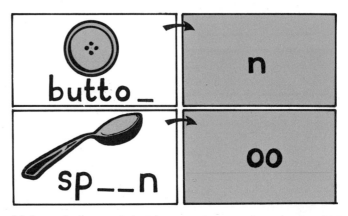

Make a similar card, but leave out a vowel, and print this on the back of the card.

Blending

The next stage in the phonic programme is to teach children how to blend sounds. Blending must be done in one of two ways, e.g. either ca-t or c-at, but *not* c-a-t. Make cards like these to illustrate blending, choosing one of the methods shown below.

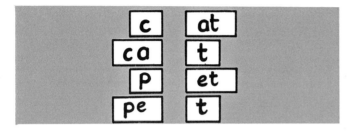

Consonant blends

Children frequently have the same trouble with blends, e.g. 'tr', as they have with the vowel digraphs and diphthongs (ai, ei, ie, oy, oa, oe, etc.). Children must learn to sound them as single units, though they may consist of two or three letters. But they are fairly regular, and this helps children to recognise them.

Exercises to help
1. Write the missing letters in the boxes.

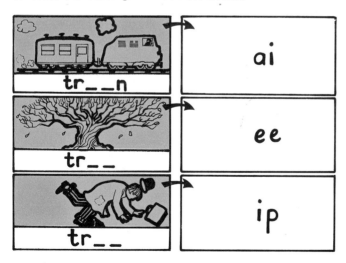

The answer is on the back of the card.

2. The children can be asked to distinguish the odd blend among a group of words which is being read out. You might try using the following words:

blood, bless, blink, band, bliss.

crib, crowd, care, crown, crystal.

trick, trip, troll, toll, tress.

plank, plinth, plimsoll, pant, place.

3. Snap cards. Make some cards like these:

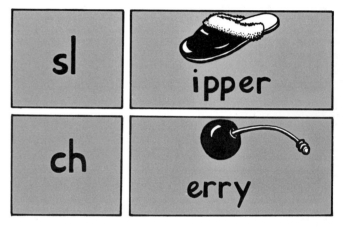

Play 'snap' by matching the two parts of each word.

4. Make some work sheets like this:

Which object has a name which begins with the letter written on the card?

Extending phonic understanding

Some children find it easier to learn lists of words or to learn a rule than to notice the letters and digraphs in a given word, or indeed to discriminate the pattern of one word from that of another. It is important to teach children to look at words in a detailed way as well as to look at their patterns.

Discrimination among word pairs
It is often helpful to use a system of rhyming when a child is reading. Instead of simply telling him a word he does not know, or asking him to spell it out, give him a clue in the form of a word which rhymes with it. When you introduce a new spelling pattern, try to relate it to the patterns the child already knows. Point out the way in which the new pattern differs from the one he knows.

e.g. hat – hate
    fat – fate
    mat – mate
    hat – hate – heat
    fat – fate – feat

The children can play games with words of this type by adding or substituting letters in given words to make 'new' words.

Structural analysis
Bring the children's attention to the structure of new words:

e.g. matchbox (match box)
    coastguard (coast guard)
    gamekeeper (game keeper)

Help the children to see the 'little words in big words' and show them that these are familiar words which they know how to spell.

They should also be encouraged to look closely at a word, to separate and to pick out syllables they know and can read, e.g. vi-sit and br-ing-ing.

Many children will be helped by exercises in using inflexional endings to make different words.

Give them some exercises like this:

The boy <u>walks</u> home.

Last night the boy _____ home.

The boy was _____ home after school.

Use letter cards to help the children build words with various inflections. Here is an example of the kind of cards you might use:

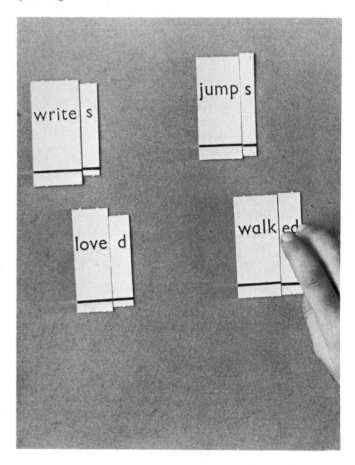

Phonic rules
Rules which can be readily applied in any situation can be useful in teaching. They can be economical in terms of learning time, and can give some children a means of solving problems.

Children playing Scrabble. This, like other word games, provides useful experience of language and good practice in spelling. The children are encouraged to expand their vocabulary by seeking new words to use in the game

Phonic generalisations of the kind which follow are very helpful. There are many other generalisations but most involve a considerable number of exceptions.

1. When 'c' and 'h' are next to each other, they make only one sound, e.g. chest, chicken, chair.

2. When the letter 'c' is followed by 'o' or 'a', the sound 'k' will be heard, e.g. camel, catch, collar, coin.

3. When 'ght' is seen in a word, the 'gh' is silent, e.g. fight, light, right, sought.

4. When a word begins with 'kn', the 'k' is silent, e.g. knee, knuckle.

5. When a word begins with 'wr', the 'w' is silent, e.g. wring, wrath, wrangle, wriggle, wrong.

6. When a word ends in 'ck' this produces the same last sound 'k', as in book, e.g. dock, sock, black.

7. When 'tion' is the final syllable in a word it stands for an unaccented 'shun' sound, e.g. collection, sanction, position.

8. Words having double 'e' usually have the long 'e' sound, e.g. beet, feet, sheep.

9. In words of one syllable which end in 'e', the vowel in the middle of the word 'says its own name', e.g. cake, bike.

10. When the letter 'i' is followed by 'gh', the 'i' stands for its long sound and the 'gh' is silent, e.g. nigh, sigh.

5 Context clues

Reading is an activity of extracting and considering meaning. This means that the first and most powerful clue to the recognition of a word is provided by the setting in which it occurs.

We have already seen how pictures can be used to help a child to understand printed words and to find out an unknown word. But the print itself also offers two groups of clues and the effective reader makes considerable use of them.

These clues are found in:

1. The use of syntax, i.e. grammatical construction.

2. The use of semantics, i.e. the meaning.

Such clues are of two types, forward acting and backward acting and both may be found within the same sentence.

Syntactic clues

A child's mastery of the grammatical construction of language is by no means complete at five years of age, but it is extensive. Even when he cannot fully understand the meaning of a sentence, he often realises that a word he cannot read has a particular function.

He might well read the following: 'John and Mary_____ in the street'.

He will realise that the unknown word must be a verb, though he will not know which one. He can thus use his memory of spoken language, and think of words like 'played', 'walked', 'danced', etc.

Semantic clues

If a reader tries to discover an unknown word on the basis of what the writer intended to say, he is making a logical appraisal of the information available to him. He has to think of all the possible words he knows and pick out the one which seems most appropriate to the context.

Though a child might successfully recognise a word by its configuration or phonic clues, he can only extend his knowledge of word meanings by understanding how to use context clues as he reads. Thus content is important both for its own sake and the clues to reading it gives to the reader.

Activities to aid development in the use of context

To begin with, try using the children's own work to teach the use of context clues. A child will know what he meant in a piece of writing, and when he reads it back he will be able to remember any words he does not immediately recognise.

Make some 'missing word' exercises with sentences from either the reader each child is using or from the children's own work.

Make cards with sentences like these, offering a number of alternative words for the child to use to fill in the gaps.

e.g. The door of the house is—blue, red, green.

I went to play—football, rounders, hopscotch—in the park.

Children often enjoy re-ordering jumbled sentences. Start by using sentences from their own written work. Next, use the words in a sentence which describes an illustration. Later, children will be able to do these puzzles without the support of pictures.

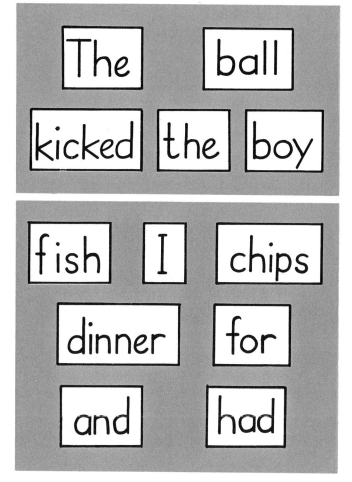

Children can play games in which they anticipate words. The teacher reads a sentence and the children must supply missing words. Each child supplies a different word for the gap. The children then decide which is the best alternative.

John played _____.

They _____all the way home from school.

Cloze procedure
Cloze procedure is a term which covers a most useful set of activities which helps children to learn to use both the syntactic and the semantic types of context clues: The principle is quite simple.

Give a child a piece of text with gaps in it. Ask the children to fill the gaps, or to close them up in order to make the passage meaningful. This can be done by omitting words at random or at evenly spaced intervals. This will help children practise using both syntactic and semantic clues, but eliminates any help from configuration or phonic clues.

Obviously there will be occasions on which a child chooses a synonym rather than the word the original text contained.

Do not treat a synonym as incorrect, but use it as a basis of discussion about the meaning of the word and whether it is appropriate to the style of the passage.

Exercises like this usually begin with a short introductory section in which no omissions occur, and go on to miss out a number of words.

 John and Jennifer went to bed early on Christmas Eve. They were excited. Their mother told them to go . . . sleep before Father Christmas came. It was dark when . . . woke up. He could see nothing, so he got . . . torch out from under the pillow. He could not believe . . . eyes. There was a great big sack which was . . . there when he went to bed. He jumped out . . . bed and went to it. How heavy it was. . . . opened the sack. It was full of the most . . . things. There were cars, books, football boots, a . . . jersey, . . . and a transistor.'

When you make exercises for children with a reading age of about ten, leave out about one word in ten. Between the reading ages of ten and thirteen, leave out about one in every seven, and over thirteen, one in every five.

Try to delete equal proportions of various parts of speech, and check that the exercise is not too difficult for the children.

On some occasions you may wish to draw rather more attention to the grammatical function of words rather than their meaning. To teach this, leave out only one part of speech from a passage, that is, leave out only nouns or only verbs. This can be a more difficult exercise than one which involves words missed out at random, or at regular intervals. Young children find it easier to replace articles, conjunctions, prepositions and pronouns than to replace nouns, verbs and adjectives, which carry the major burden of meaning.

Cloze procedure can be used in a form where some phonic and/or configuration clues are also retained in a passage. Any of the following ideas or indeed combinations of them could be used within a text, e.g. the space left by the word 'collar' could be depicted in the following ways.

c_____   initial letter only

c_ _ _ _ _   initial letter plus the number of letters in the word

_____r   final letter only

_ _ _ _ _r   final letter plus the number of letters in the word

_ _ll_ _   medial letters plus the number of letters in the word

____ll_____   medial letters only.

Cloze procedure can be made less of a formal exercise and become even more helpful to the teacher if it is used as a basis for group discussion.

Here all the children in a group use the same passage. At first the children tackle the passage alone, each child making his individual response in the spaces. The group meets and wherever different words have been placed in the same space each child must argue the case for his own word. When everyone agrees, the different words are compared with the author's original words, and more discussion takes place.

Most of these later discussions will turn upon subtleties of meaning and style though just occasionally children will find they have made grammatical errors.

Another idea is to replace key words with a nonsense syllable. This is particularly helpful for learning the con-

cepts associated with words, shades of meaning, summary words and synonyms. These are very useful as a basis for discussion in a group.

Multiple meanings
Words with multiple meanings are numerous in English and children must learn how to test various meanings of one word within a given context to gain a more adequate clue to another word

e.g. They run down the road.

Run the engine for five minutes.

Your credit has run out.

He is to run the new supermarket.

Synonyms and antonyms
An author often uses a synonym or an antonym to give emphasis to a point.

If the child becomes aware that words such as 'and', 'or', 'neither_____nor', 'both_____and' can be used to signal that words of this type are about to appear this will often help him to guess the meaning of a word he does not know.

e.g. Where 'friends' is unknown: 'Mary and Joan like each other, and have become firm friends.'

Where 'prosperous' is unknown: 'Neither the poor nor the prosperous failed to find a welcome at the bishop's home.'

Often, an author uses a summary word or phrase to emphasise a point. Such a word may often be unfamiliar to a child.

Exercise in working out the meaning of a word by looking at the rest of the sentence will help a child to remember the word so that he can use it in future.

e.g. 'She was never invited to parties, everyone ignored her in the corridors and she soon realised that she was being *ostracised*.'

'The object was very *buoyant* for it was bouncing up and down in the water.'

6 Working out which skills a child needs to learn

How to work out which skills are needed

The most effective way of doing this is to hear the child read regularly. This activity will show you a child's strengths and weaknesses, his use of configuration, of context, of pictorial clues, and how he applies his phonic skills.

It is extremely important to remember to let the child make mistakes, to give him time to try and correct them and to observe how he goes about doing this. For example if a child reads: 'He rode the house' (instead of 'horse') you will know that he is not using his knowledge of semantics, secondly he is not applying his knowledge of context which properly used should help him to make sense, and thirdly he has not applied his phonic skills. For example, reading 'house' for 'horse' could indicate to you that

1. He may be using four letters to guide him.

2. He has matched the similar configuration of horse to house.

3. He needs to be trained to look more carefully at the position of medial letters in a word.

4. He needs to learn the 'or' sound.

5. The child is simply failing to read for meaning.

Errors and how they can help
Use a sheet of paper with the following headings. You can use this to make records of the errors children make and to work out the best way to help the child overcome his reading problems.

Substitutions: a good sign if they make sense semantically or syntactically.

Omissions: might be a sign of perceptual trouble.

No response: a lack of confidence.

Repetitions: a lack of confidence.

Self-correction: a good sign, suggests that he is receiving help from the visual input or context.

Insertion: a good sign if by doing this he makes a sentence approximate to his own linguistic patterns.

There are other errors which are to do with failure to recognise letters:

Initial errors involving consonants or vowels: e.g. agg for egg, flight for light

Reversal of letters: e.g. dun for bun

Inversion of letters: e.g. pun for bun

Mid vowel errors: e.g. sat for sit

Serial distortion of letters: e.g. its for sit

Reversal of whole words: e.g. nub for bun

Errors in initial consonant blends: e.g. tank for thank

Errors in final consonant blends: e.g. thick for think

Errors in vowel digraphs: e.g. bok for book

It is not always clear why a child makes mistakes when

he is reading aloud. It is best to discuss the problems with the child.

Suggestions to help to correct reading errors

Substitution: Concentrate on phonic analysis. Give the child easier reading material.

Omissions of words: Insist on emphasising meaning. Ask the child to read with you. Use flash cards with incomplete sentences and complete ones for comparison.

Repetitions: Train the child in methods of attacking new words.

Read aloud with the child. Encourage the child to read more slowly and calmly.

Reversals: Emphasise the direction of reading by giving the child exercises involving tracing words. Try pointing to the words or underlining them while the child is reading.

Omissions of lines: Make sure the lines are spaced well apart. Try giving the child a piece of card to put under the line of text he is reading. He should move it down one line every time he reaches the end of a line.

Record keeping

It is important to record your assessment of a child's progress through his reading. This is particularly encouraging for him, but you must also keep a record of his errors and your ideas for correcting him.

Make cards like these for your records.

READING RECORD CARD

Name Sarah Jones
Class ~~I~~ II
Date of Birth 12·3·67
Sight ✓
Hearing ✓

	Date		Date		Date	
Reading age	6/73	6·9	6/74	8·8		
Test used	Burt		Burt			
Reading quotient	101		110			
Comprehension age	7·2		9·0			
Test used	Neale		Neale			

Reading Schemes (list of books, supplementaries and library books completed)
Ladybird , Time for Reading

Books	Date	Books	Date	Books	Date	Books	Date
1a, 1b	5/73, 7/73	Cherry Family	2/74	Doggo	9/74	5a, 5b, 5c	6/75
1c, 2a	9/73, 10/73	Eight Quickies	3/74	As tall as a Giraffe	10/74	6a	
		3a, 3b, 3c	4/74-6/74	4a, 4b	1/75		
2b, 2c	11/73	The Naughty Twins	7/74	4c	3/75		

Skills	Weaknesses	Materials used	Date
Visual discrimination	✓		
Auditory discrimination	✓		
Phonics	unsure of vowel digraphs	Stott - Half Moon Cards Philip Tacey Word Building SRA Lab. 1c.	7/75
Context	needs practice		
Comprehension (literal, inferential, evaluative)	inferential level	matching newspaper headlines with print.	9/75

Reading Problems   Details of diagnosis, tests used action taken.

7 Teaching word attack skills through games

The value of games

Children can learn from organised play. There are many games which teach word attack skills.

Do not over-use games as some children will have had enough of them and will become bored. Games are not a scheme in themselves, and they should be made to fit into your reading programme and to supplement it at appropriate points. For example, if you feel some children need extra practice with the recognition of initial letters, then you should organise a game which helps with this.

You should make sure that the children are actually learning and that they can apply what they learn to a real reading situation. There can be a very real danger if you are not careful, that children can play games just for the games' sake when really you want them to develop a specific reading skill.

Some useful games are produced commercially.

However, some of the most effective games can be those which you make yourself. Making your own games can not only help you to develop and deepen your own insight into the nature of the learning, but is also more likely to result in a piece of apparatus more suitably tailored to meet the needs of your own class.

Building a sight vocabulary with whole words

If you are going to try this, select words from the child's spoken vocabulary, or choose key words.

Hop Scotch

This is a game designed to teach recognition of whole words.

The game can be played in a hall or playground. Draw squares and write words in them. Call out the words and ask a child to jump into the square which has the word written in it. You help children to learn to tell the difference between left and right by asking them to begin at the top left hand corner and to keep on going left to right. You could also have several sets of teams with different lists of words written in the squares.

Pairs

This is the simple game of pelmanism using word cards instead of ordinary playing cards. Make several pairs of cards, and put them all face downwards. Each child takes it in turn to turn over two cards. If he finds two which match, the child keeps the cards and has another turn. If they do not match it is the next child's turn. When all the cards have been picked up, each child should see how many he has. The child with the most cards is the winner.

Football

Make out a board like the one shown opposite. Now make a pack of ten flash cards using words from a reading scheme. Put the cards face downwards.

Choose two teams, and use a dice to decide who starts first. The children then take it in turns in alternating teams, to turn the flash cards over and try to read them. If a child can read the word he may put the card on his opponents' part of the field. The team which ends the game with the most cards in its opponents' part of the field wins. This game can be used as a diagnostic and teaching instrument.

Sight vocabulary—ladder game

This is a game for any number of children. Make cards like the one shown below and some flash cards. Each child has a counter. The children try to read the flash cards. They work one at a time. Every time a child reads a word correctly his counter is moved up the ladder. If he fails, his counter is not moved. The first to reach the top wins. The words selected may be the sight words from your reading scheme or taken from a list which you think might be useful.

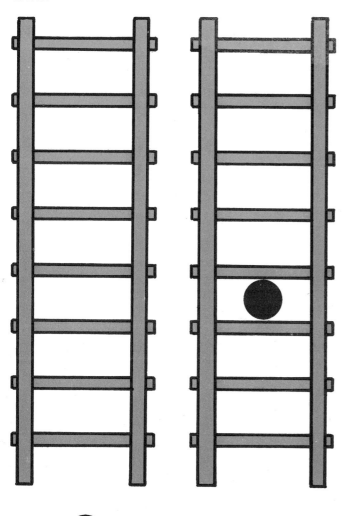

Word recognition

Chase

The children form a circle with their hands behind their backs. One child is 'man'. He shows the other children a card with a word on it. He puts the card into one child's hand, and calls the word. The child with the card chases 'man' and has to catch him.

The game is repeated using different cards and different children as 'man'.

Above: The child from the middle of the circle puts a card into another child's hand and calls out the word. Below: The second child chases the first

Two teams

Write two lists of identical words on the blackboard, one for each team. The two lists, however, should not be in the same order. The children are numbered in pairs, 1, 2, 3, 4 and so on. When the teacher calls out a word the first pair point to their word. The child who is first gets a point. The team with the largest number of points wins.

Tiddleywinks

Write some words on a board like the one shown opposite. Use words which have the positive value of teaching such things as visual discrimination or pnonic blends. Each child has to flick a counter into the word space and be able to read the word. You can stick new words on the board if you want to change it, or use acetate to make the board and write on it with a chinagraph pencil.

Initial letters

Man from space

One child is 'man'. The other children in the class call out

An example of the kind of board used for tiddleywinks

'Man from space, can we chase?' He replies: 'Yes, if your name begins the same way as "jug" or "window".'

Any children whose names begin with these letters chase 'man'. The child who catches him becomes the new 'man'.

Letter recognition

Find the letter

This game is played in the same way as 'Two teams' (see this page) except that letters rather than words are used. Use both lower and upper case letters.

Phonic games

Vowel sounds: tag

Ten children are divided into two teams. Each child in a team carries a different vowel written on a card.

The teacher calls out a word which begins with one of the initial vowel sounds the children are holding. The children who have these letters run to touch the ball. First to touch the ball wins.

Vowel digraphs: crosswords

Ask the children to fill in the gaps on a sheet like this:

Blending: syllables

Words of two syllables are written on tinted cards. The first syllable is printed on a yellow card and the second on a green one. The yellow cards are dealt to the players, who then take turns to pick up a green one to see if they can blend the two cards to make a word.

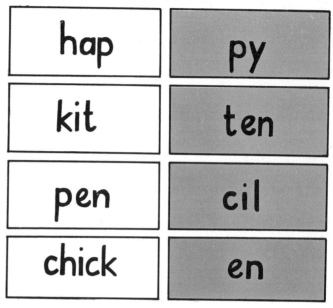

Polysyllabic words can be learnt by using the same rules. You need to have a sufficient supply of tinted card to match the number of syllables, e.g. for words of three syllables you could use yellow, green and red cards.

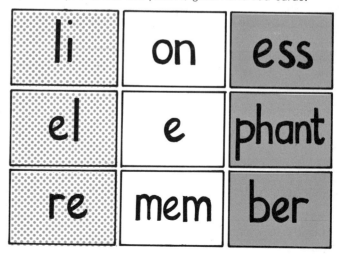

Helping a child to keep her eyes on the right line of print as she reads (see page 24). The same card can be used to record mistakes as the child reads. Keep the cards in a box or a tin and refer back to them when you next hear the child reading

Children should learn to read feeling that the task is both enjoyable and useful. If they have this attitude to reading, they will soon begin to seek out books and read them for pleasure

Appendix

Useful books for the teacher

The Teaching of Reading by Donald Moyle, published by Ward Lock Educational

Aids to Reading by John M. Hughes, published by Evans Brothers

Phonics and the Teaching of Reading by John M. Hughes, published by Evans Brothers

Reading and Remedial Reading by A. E. Tansley, published by Routledge & Kegan Paul

The Standard Reading Tests by J. C. Daniels and H. Diack, published by Hart Davis Educational

Get Reading Right by S. Jackson, published by Gibson

The Assessment of Reading Skills by J. Turner, published by the United Kingdom Reading Association

Dictionaries

My Book of Words by T. J. and J. A. Hulme, published by A. and C. Black Ltd

Black's Reading Dictionary, published by A. and C. Black Ltd

Picture Dictionary, compiled by Lavinia Derwent, published by Burke Books. This is a useful beginner's dictionary which has been especially designed to help children who are learning to read

Young Set Dictionaries published by Chambers. A graded series of four dictionaries

Words Children Want to Use by Amy L. Brown, John Downing and John Sceats, published by Chambers. This is a handbook to the *Young Set Dictionaries*

My First Golden Dictionary, published by Hamlyn. Contains definitions of 1,030 words for children aged six to eight years

Key Words First Picture Dictionary, and *Key Words Second Picture Dictionary*, published by Ladybird. The first of these dictionaries contains 93 key words. The second contains 300 words

Children's Working Dictionary by Arthur J. Arkely, published by Thomas Nelson and Sons Ltd. This book contains definitions of 4,000 words as well as puzzles and exercises

An Easy Dictionary, published by Schofield and Sims. Contains definitions of 5,000 words for children aged seven to nine

Look it Up, published by Schofield and Sims. A companion book of exercises for *An Easy Dictionary*

Thorndike Junior Illustrated Dictionary compiled by E. L. Thorndike, published by Hodder and Stoughton Educational. Defines nearly 25,000 of the most commonly used words

A First Practice Dictionary by O. B. Gregory, published by A. Wheaton and Company. The book is designed for children of average ability in the seven to eight age groups, but can be used by all children who are learning how to use a dictionary for the first time

Books for phonic work

Phonic Workbooks by E. H. Grassam, published by Ginn and Company Ltd. There are six individual books identified by their numbers

Sounds and Words by Vera Southgate and J. Havenhand, published by Hodder and Stoughton Educational. A six-book series of books for the classroom accompanied by a teacher's book

Sound Sense (*Books 1–8*) by A. E. Tansley, published by E. J. Arnold and Son Ltd. A series of books providing systematic instruction in phonic analysis

Taped reading programmes and programmes for phonic work

Bell & Howell A-V Ltd, Alperton House, Bridge-water Road, Wembley, Middlesex HA0 1EG

Language Masters — a simple magnetic recorder using audio-visual work cards. The teacher can record on one track words or sentences and incorporate pictures and tests on the cards

Model 701 — mains operated, with record/playback on master and student tracks

Model 717BX — has the same basic facilities as Model 701, with the following additional facilities: 'Piano-key' controls, manual half-speed facility, instant repeat facility, separate microphone/headphone sockets for use with boom microphone/headset

Model 1727 — battery operated with playback on master track and record/playback on student track

Accessories — headphones, boom microphone headset (for use with Model 717BX only), four-way Junction Box

Programmes — Work Study (a junior phonics programme), Ladybird Key Words Card Set, Magic Roundabout Reading Scheme, Find The Word (a dictionary skills kit), Word Blending (covers single consonant/vowel blends),

Let's Speak English, Words in Action (a reading development programme for remedial pupils in the 13–16 age group), Programme Building Kit (a set of 200 blank cards in four sizes)

E. J. Arnold and Son Ltd, Butterly Street, Leeds LS10 1AX

Listening to Sounds 2BC — recorded by A. E. Tansley. This material is for use in preparatory work on sound patterns. Later recordings use material from *Sound Sense* (see this page)

Remedial Supply Company, Dixon Street, Wolverhampton WV2 2BX

Phonics 1 — covers single sounds, phonic blending and early digraphs. There are tapes 1 and 2, and two workbooks which are bought separately

Phonics 2 — covers simple and complex blending of sounds and putting syllables together. There are about 250 words, each matched with an illustration. There are twenty lessons in all, taking from 20–30 minutes each. There are two tapes, and two workbooks

Phonics 1A — is an extended version of Phonics 1. There are twelve lessons instead of six. There is a tape, Phonics 1A, and a set of 12 sheets

The Phonic Blending Tapes — these are tapes for Phonic Blending Books 1–5 — There are expendable workbooks, which show words broken into sound patterns

The Letter Shifting Sequences — this is a tape which is used to show how words can be altered by moving and changing one letter at a time. Other apparatus needed here is plastic letters and digraphs

Attacking New Words — is a series of tape kits in three stages, starting with the 5–6 age group and going on to reinforcing phonic work and extending vocabulary

Listening Tapes — two tapes with four sets of six sounds each, making 48 sounds altogether. The cassette version has one cassette only. To improve the very early level sounds from the environment are used. Picture material and sheets for playing listening Lotto are also provided.

The Sound Discrimination Tapes — there are two tapes and the material is an expendable work pad. This is designed to help the child to discriminate speech sounds more acutely

N.B. All tapes made by the Remedial Supply Company are also available as cassettes

Commercially produced games and equipment for teaching whole words

Macdonald Educational Ltd, Holywell House, Worship Street, London EC2

Happy Words — a card game designed to help with reading and spelling throughout the primary school. It covers the vital areas of the teaching of phonics

Wordmaster Major — a set of visually exciting games which provide practice in word recognition, spelling and the formation of sentences. The kit contains fourteen pupil cards, a teacher's control sheet and a set of counters

Shapemaster Minor — this game is designed to help children to master basic geometric shapes. Coloured squares, ovals, etc are used to teach children to match shape to shape and to help them to verbalise their recognition of shapes and to abstract the appropriate concepts. For children ages two to eight

Philip & Tacey Ltd, North Way, Andover, Hampshire

Discrimination Picture and Shape Sorting Cards — for a reception class or slow learners. Six boxes, each containing nine sets of three matching cards

Letter Recognition and Sorting Strip Books — children match letters in threes. Two sets of four books

Early Word Picture and Word Matching Cards — 240 subjects distributed over 12 boxes

Sentence Completion Reading Games — exercises in reading and comprehension for two, three or four players. The first part of each sentence is printed on a card of one colour and the second on a card of another colour. Two sets of 48 cards

Invicta Plastics Ltd, Educational Aids Division, Oadby, Leicestershire LE2 4LB

Lingo — this game is played in groups rather like Bingo. It provides practice in identifying letters and letter groups both visually and orally, and how these link to form words.

Thomas Hope Ltd, St Philip's Drive, Royton, Oldham OL2 6AG

Lexicon — a spelling game. This game is distributed by Thomas Hope Ltd., but not manufactured by them

Kiddicraft — this game is designed to help children to learn to read and spell. It contains a collection of 300 common words

Science Research Associates, Newtown Road, Henley on Thames, Oxfordshire RG9 1EW

Word Games (Reading Laboratory 1) — contains 44 word building/word recognition games to develop word attack skills

James Galt and Sons Ltd, Brookfield Road, Cheadle, Cheshire

Picture Word Lotto — a group game to build up vocabulary. It extends the activity of simple picture matching to include sight-word learning and word to word matching. Four boards and 36 pictures in a box

Picture-Word Matching Cards — this game teaches sight words in association with pictures and is extended to include direct word-to-word matching using the reverse side of the picture. There are four sets, each with ten picture/word cards

The Colour Learning Game — a simple game which encourages colour matching and the recognition of the names of twelve colours

Basic Words Lotto — the 12 most useful words. Four baseboards and 48 question cards

Key Words Lotto 1 — a game which gives practice in the 20 next most used words. Four baseboards and 80 question cards

Key Words Lotto 2 — the 48 most used nouns. Each of the four baseboards contains 12 different words. Four baseboards and 48 question cards

Key Words Lotto 3 — 72 key words on four baseboards. There are 18 different words per card. Four baseboards and 72 question cards

Key Words Self Teaching Cards — one to eight children can use these self corrective cards at the same time. Sixty-four words, mostly nouns, are presented. Every baseboard has eight words which correspond with those on the eight word/picture cards for use with it.

Word Building Box — a strong plastic box with a folding lid with rails for word making

One hundred alphabet capitals and 100 alphabet lower case letters are also available

Oppositions — in working through these cards a child learns the correct use of prepositions and adjectives in conjunction with their opposites in increasingly complex contexts. Three colour coded baseboards, each with 12 word/picture cards in a box

Initial Blends — these cards provide a means of learning the important initial consonant blends. Two boxes, each with three colour coded sets of four paired cards

Hart Davis Educational, Granada Publishing, 29 Frogmore, St Albans, Hertfordshire AI2 2NF

Family Pairs — a game for two or more players which involves collecting similar words as the title suggests

More Family Pairs — an extension of *Family Pairs*

It's Fun to Read — a games pack which can be used as supplementary reading material

Commercially produced games and equipment for teaching phonics

E. J. Arnold and Son Ltd (see page 33 for address)

Spellmaster — for spelling and reading practice

Shakewords — a spelling game played with 14 lettered discs.

Tum-a-word — three solid cubes with letters printed on four sides. These can be turned over individually to make 45 words

Hart-Davis Educational (see this page for address)

Phonic Pairs — a game for two or more children, useful to all who have had some phonic training, especially older children who are slow readers

Phonic Sets — a game for two or more children which gives practice in the quick recognition of identical word beginnings

I Spy — a game for two or more players which gives practice in recognising initial sounds. A letter is printed on one side of a card and a picture giving a clue to the sound is printed on the other

Pair It — this game is for two or more players. It gives practice in sounding the common final single consonants.

Match It — matching the sounds in word endings

Make It — a word making game

Ginn and Company Ltd, Elsinore House, Buckingham Street, Aylesbury, Bucks HP20 2NQ

Sounds and Words — a set of cards which can be used with baseboards for a wide range of phonic activities

Time for Sounds — four workbooks which introduce phonics and may be used in conjunction with phonic workbooks (see page 33)

James Galt and Sons Ltd (see page 34 for address)

Sound Links — cards which enable a child to assimilate some simple rules of word construction. The child selects the correct ending for the incomplete word which is denoted by a clear illustration. The cards include 'the silent b', vowel digraphs, as well as consonant blends and digraphs. Three boxes each containing three colour coded sets each of four paired cards

Picture Word Dominoes — all the words in this game are phonically regular, so this game provides excellent practice for children who are just beginning to build words. Two colour coded sets of 20 cards in a box

Picture Letter Matching Cards — colourfully illustrated cards which enable children to learn the sounds of all the letters of the alphabet except x. Set of 25 paired cards in a box.

Phonic Self-teacher — twenty-eight sounds including all those of the letters of the alphabet, are taught with this self corrective apparatus. It can be used by up to seven children at the same time. Seven baseboards and 56 coloured cards

Rhyming Pairs — children learn important word elements by associating pairs of rhyming words. As a first stage, the child uses a picture clue. As a second stage, the child uses the reverse of the cards. Box 1 deals with phonically regular three letter words, Box 2 with final consonant blends and digraphs

Word Patterns — this employs the principle of rhyming vocabulary to teach some important basic word forms. Box 1 deals with phonically regular three letter words, and Box 2 deals with 'the silent e' and final consonant clusters. Each box contains two colour coded sets each of nine paired cards

Phonic Practice Cards — two sets, each of six large folding cards, make between them nearly 200 words in large print in selected word groupings

Word Maker — apparatus to help children to learn to link words to make new words. They can make a large number of known words as well as fantasy words which lead to imaginative language use

Build-a-word — simple words illustrating certain spelling principles are built up letter by letter on a baseboard using letter cards matched to picture cues. Three boxes each containing three colour coded baseboards each with 16 letter cards

Sentence Building Cards — a set of cards with 118 specially chosen words which give children the opportunity to create interesting and humorous sentences

Philip & Tacey Ltd (see page 34 for address)

Scholar's Alphabet Sorting Tray — a durable box with a plastic insert with 28 divisions marked in small and capital letters

Primary Plastic 1½" Letters — these are all lower case. There is one set in which all the letters are blue and another in which all the vowels are red and all the consonants blue

Unilock Plastic Word-making Letters — these are used for word and sentence building. There are 49 pieces, lettered on both sides. The set has lower case and capital letters, two full stops, a question mark and six blanks for word spaces

Consonant-Vowel Blend Matching Cards — each set contains 2 boxes of 16 picture and word combinations. Self-corrective

Sussex Vowel Sorting and Word Cards — 24 matching cards. The box displays five vowels. This is an audio-visual task for the early stages of reading

Sort and Sound Vowel Digraph Cards — these introduce children to the most common medial vowel digraphs. Each box has nine puzzles. Set of four boxes

Invicta Plastics Ltd (see page 34 for address)

Letter Group Set — a word building set which includes diphthongs and digraphs. It consists of tablets pegged to fit into a black peg board which is provided

ESA Creative Learning Ltd, Pinnacles, PO Box 22, Harlow, Essex CM19 5AY

The 'Look, I'm Reading' programme — this is a new reading scheme which is built up in logical sections, taking the child from basic recognition of the sounds of letters to the advanced stage of reading of about six years. The programme consists of the following 'units':

Unit 1 Alphabet Cards — a set of 44 cards and 660 word and picture strips

Unit 2 Envelopes of Picture and Word Cards — 440

picture and word cards

Unit 3   Window Books — 20 different books

Unit 4   Alphabet Children Books — a pack of five books using pictorial clues to the letters of the alphabet

Unit 5   Sentence Books — pack of 10 books covering the letters A–Z. Printed letters to make up words used in the scheme. Pictures for sounds-sets to introduce sounds of the letters of the alphabet. There are a number of other items included in Unit 5 and all items are available separately

Alphabet Poster Cards — 26 large cards in full colour with an illustration and the alphabetical letter

Locking Letters — large wooden interlocking beech blocks with clear script letters printed on them

Junior Scrabble — a word and picture scrabble set containing two games

Scrabble

Alphabet Play Tray — the letters of the alphabet for young children. A strong wooden board and pieces

Alphabet Lotto — this includes cards featuring lower case letters for up to six players and a callers master card

Except where stated the addresses given in this list are those of the makers of games and equipment, who will supply catalogues describing their equipment and information about it. Many makers have numbered their goods in their catalogues and expect these numbers to be quoted when items are ordered. It is always a good idea to study the catalogue before ordering anything.

Teaching 5-13 Teachers' Units

Advisory editor: **Frank F. Blackwell**
General Inspector for Schools, London Borough of Croydon and Director of the Primary Extension Programme of the Council for Educational Technology

Teaching 5–13 is a range of books that reflect current development in education in practical terms. It provides sources of immediate help to teachers, with the liberal use of photographs and diagrams to convey information.

The range of books in Teaching 5–13 will be wide enough to illustrate both changes in emphasis and curriculum content as the child develops over the years between five and thirteen. At present, *Teaching 5–13* comprises three series: **Projects, Reading, Mathematics.**

Projects

Consultant editor: **Frank F. Blackwell**

Each book in this series covers a specific topic and contains a collection of projects relevant to that topic. All the projects are easy to organise. They will appeal to teachers with little experience of project work.

Bakery	356 04883 7	**Giants, witches and dragons**	356 04885 3
Flight	356 04884 5	**North American Indians**	356 04886 1

Reading

Consultant editor: **Donald Moyle**
Reader in Education, Edge Hill College of Higher Education

Though this topic has been split into a number of short books, the series has a unity of thinking. The books form a compendium of activities, apparatus and games for reading and language development from pre-school to adolescence.

Towards reading	356 05025 4	**Word attack skills**	356 05055 6
Reading teacher's source book	356 05054 8	**Beginning to read**	356 05056 4

Mathematics

Consultant editor: **Frank F. Blackwell**
Written by **Malcolm Currie,** Headmaster, Sylvan High School, Croydon, and **Leslie Foster,** Headmaster, Benson Infant and Junior School, Croydon

These books give an overall picture of modern mathematics in the Primary context. The books are based upon the child's developmental stages. So, although it is not possible to use chronological as the basis of organisation, it is useful to indicate an average age level for each stage: Book 1, 0–5 years; Book 2, 5–7 years; Book 3, 7–9 years; Book 4, 9–11 years; Books 5 and 6, 11–13 years.

		In preparation	
1 Play's the thing	356 05063 7	**3 Sets the scene**	356 05065 3
2 Classes and counts	356 05064 5	**4 Physical structures**	356 05066 1

38

Science 5-13 Teachers' Units

Sponsored by The Schools Council, The Nuffield Foundation and The Scottish Education Department

The *Science 5–13* Project has a new and important way of looking at the problem of helping children between the ages of five and thirteen to learn about science. Its trial materials were thoroughly tested in the schools of 27 local education authorities throughout Great Britain.

The principal aim of the teaching ideas and objectives set out in the *Science 5–13* Units is the development in children of an enquiring mind and a scientific approach to problems. The Project recognises that attitudes of enquiry, objective judgement, personal responsibility and ability to work and organise one's work independently can be established in children at an early age.

The books form a series of Units to which teachers can turn for sound advice and guidance, for starting points and background information, when children are working in subject areas covered by the books.

With objectives in mind	356 04009 7	
Early experiences	356 04005 4	
Working with wood: Stages 1 & 2	356 04011 9	
Working with wood: Background information	356 04010 0	
Time: Stages 1 & 2 and background	356 04008 9	
Science from toys: Stages 1 & 2 and background	356 04006 2	
Science, models and toys: Stage 3	356 04351 7	
Structures and forces: Stages 1 & 2	356 04007 0	
Structures and forces: Stage 3	356 04107 7	
Holes, gaps and cavities: Stages 1 & 2	356 04108 5	
Metals: Stages 1 & 2	356 04103 4	
Metals: background information	356 04104 2	
Change: Stages 1 & 2 and background	356 04105 0	
Change: Stage 3	356 04346 0	
Minibeasts: Stages 1 & 2	356 04106 9	
Trees: Stages 1 & 2	356 04347 9	
Coloured things: Stages 1 & 2	356 04348 7	
Ourselves: Stages 1 & 2	356 04349 5	
Like and unlike: Stages 1, 2 & 3	356 04350 9	
Children and plastics: Stages 1 & 2 and background	356 04352 5	

Using the Environment by Margaret Collis

1 Early explorations 356 04353 3

2 Investigations
Part 1   356 04354 1
Part 2   356 04355 X

3 Tackling problems
Part 1   356 04356 8
Part 2   356 05000 9

4 Ways and means   356 05001 7

This teachers' compendium of field studies for children aged 5 to 13 completes the *Science 5–13* Project. It has been designed to show teachers how they can help children to develop enquiring minds through a gradual extension of their experience of outdoor exploration and of the practical work arising from this when they return to school.

All the material has been closely related to children's development and much information about organisation of outdoor studies, techniques and equipment has been included.

Teaching Primary Science

Teacher's Units

A Chelsea College project sponsored by the Nuffield Foundation
and the Social Science Research Council

This series is designed to provide support and guidance to practising teachers and student teachers who are about to teach simple science in primary schools. Those who have had little or no scientific training will find the books invaluable. They can also be used by lecturers as resource material in science curriculum courses in colleges of education and in in-service work.

The project consists of a series of generously illustrated units of work and a guide which describes the philosophy of them and deals specifically with different methods and approaches suitable for college and in-service courses in primary science. The method of concentrating in each unit on a particular topic or area of work greatly increases the confidence of the practising teacher or student teacher in handling science. It adds to the ease and enjoyment of their teaching and encourages self-help in extending their scientific knowledge. And it ensures a quick and proper understanding of *what* science is, *why* science should be taught, and *how* science should be taught.

Candles	356 05070 X	**Paints and materials**	356 05075 0
Seeds and seedlings	356 05072 6	**Fibres and fabrics**	356 05076 9
Science from waterplay	356 05071 8	**Mirrors and magnifiers**	356 05078 5